A N T S

Published by Smart Apple Media

123 South Broad Street

Mankato, Minnesota 56001

Photos: Dan L. Perlman (cover, pages 2-3, 6-11, 13-30);

Entomological Society of America/Ries Memorial Slide

Collection (pages 4-5, 12)

Design &Production: EvansDay Design

Project management: Odyssey Books

Library of Congress Cataloging-in-Publication Data

Halfmann, Janet, 1944–

Ants / Janet Halfmann. - 1st ed.

p. cm. – (Bugs)

Includes bibliographical references and index.

Summary: Describes the habitat, life cycle, behavior,

predators, and unique characteristics of various species

of ants.

ISBN 1-887068-29-5 (alk. paper)

1. Ants–Juvenile literature.   [1. Ants.] I. Title

II. Series: Bugs (Mankato, Minn.)

QL568.F7H29 1998

595.79'6–dc21   98-5838

First Edition   9 8 7 6 5 4 3 2 1

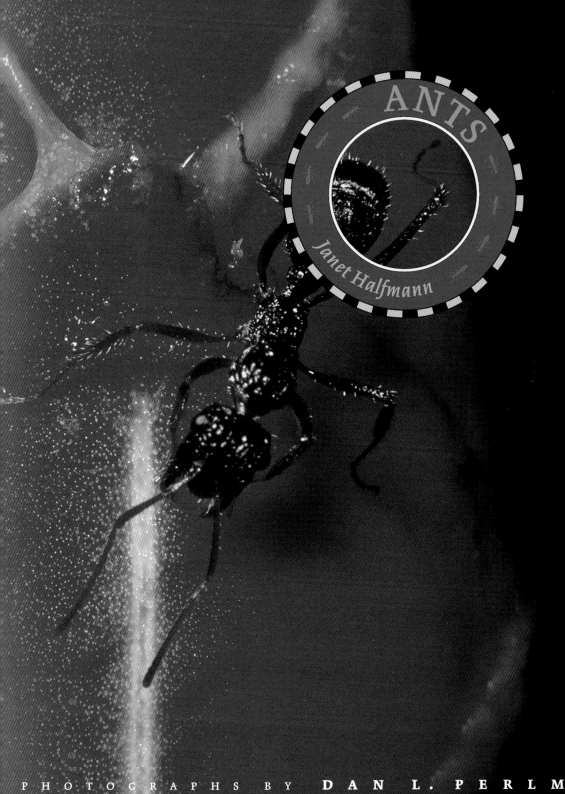

ANTS

Janet Halfmann

PHOTOGRAPHS BY **DAN L. PERLMAN**

IMAGINE WALKING THROUGH A JUNGLE

WHEN UP AHEAD ON THE PATH YOU SEE A

LONG, NARROW RIBBON OF SOMETHING

BLACK. AS YOU GET CLOSER, YOU SEE THE

RIBBON IS MOVING. BUT IT'S NOT A SNAKE;

IT'S A TRAIL OF *army ants!* THOUSANDS ARE

ON THE MARCH, *killing* AND **DEVOURING**

ANY CREATURE SMALL ENOUGH TO ATTACK.

YOUR FRIEND *grabs* YOUR ARM AND SAYS,

"*DON'T GO NEAR,* FOR IF THEY GET ON YOU..." THESE ARE KNOWN AS *KILLER ANTS,* OR ECITON BURCHELLI, TO SCIENTISTS. **FIERCE** HUNTERS, THEIR ARMIES *stream* ACROSS THE JUNGLE FLOOR OF TROPICAL AMERICA, KILLING ALL THE PREY THEY MEET. EVEN LARGER CREATURES SUCH AS *tarantulas, lizards,* AND *young birds* **DON'T STAND A CHANCE.**

The Ant's Family

Ants are everywhere, and in amazing numbers. Lean against a tree anywhere in the world, and the first insect to crawl on you is likely to be an ant. And it won't be just one, but several. For no ant can live alone. It depends upon a family.

Ants belong to the ORDER, or group, of insects called *Hymenoptera*, which means "membrane wings." This is because the young queens and males have wings. Other members of this order include bees and wasps.

Many Hymenoptera are SOCIAL insects. That means they live and work together in a community. The ants' community is called a COLONY.

The ants' family name is *Formicidae*. Ants have been around for 100 million years. They have been living on the earth since the time of the dinosaurs.

The Queen's Family   Within the colony, each ant has a special position called a CASTE. There are three major ant castes: queens, workers, and soldiers. The QUEEN is the largest and most important ant in the colony. She is its mother and founder. Each colony has one or more queens. The queen lays all the eggs for the colony. A *Myrmica rubra* queen will lay as few as 400 eggs per year, but the queen army ant will lay a whopping 2 million eggs yearly!

Most queens live five years or more, but some species have much shorter lives. The queen of a colony of tiny Pharaoh's ants lives only three months. At the other extreme, a *Lasius niger* queen

This male army ant has wings, as do most males. Most young queens also have wings. They fly only at mating time.

Trillions of Ants

You wouldn't want the job of counting the ants. Scientists estimate that 1,000 trillion ants are alive in the world at any one time! There are more ants than any other animal.

Ant colonies vary from a few dozen workers to a million or more. A colony of *Formica yessensis* found in Japan had 306 million workers and 1 million queens living in 45,000 interconnected nests extending across 675 acres (273 hectares)!

This large bullet ant worker in Costa Rica carries a drop of water in her jaws.

lovingly tended in a laboratory nest lived a record 29 years!

The WORKERS take care of the queen, her babies, and the nest. They are all females. The youngest workers generally stay inside the nest. They feed the queen, take care of the babies, store the food, and clean the nest. The older workers expand the nest and go out to search for food. Workers generally live only a few weeks or months.

Some species have special workers called SOLDIERS. They have large heads and extra-strong jaws. Their job is to defend the colony. The sharp jaws of leafcutter soldiers can cut through leather!

Habitat

There are 9,500 known SPECIES, or kinds, of ants, but scientists believe there are thousands more. Ants live on all continents except Antarctica. They are most common in tropical regions, such as in Latin America and Africa.

North America has about 600 species. One of the largest and most common is *Camponotus pennsylvanicus*. Called the black carpenter ant, it makes its nest in wood. Also familiar is the little black ant *(Monomorium minimum)*. It is often found in homes and likes sweet things and human food.

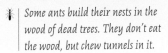

Some ants build their nests in the wood of dead trees. They don't eat the wood, but chew tunnels in it.

The rough harvester ant *(Pogonomyrmex rugosus)*, which eats seeds and grains, is common in the southwestern United States. In the southern United States, the red imported fire ant *(Solenopsis invicta)* is well known for its painful stings and the large mounds it builds in fields.

All Kinds of Nests Most species of ants, such as the little black ant, dig their nests underground. Several species, including the wood ant, build large mounds of dirt, twigs, or pine needles over their underground nests. Carpenter ants chew tunnels in the damp, rotten wood of logs or telephone poles, and sometimes even houses. Tropical weaver ants build nests of leaves and silk high up in trees in the rain forest.

The inside of the ants' nest is damp and has many hallways and rooms. There is a chamber for the queen and nurseries for the eggs and baby ants. Other rooms are used to store or grow food. The workers constantly enlarge the nest and keep it spotless.

These mounds were made by leafcutter ants digging a large nest underground.

The Ant Menu

Ants like a variety of foods. Army ants eat insects and other animals. Harvester ants eat seeds. Fire ants eat both animals and plants. Many species, including black garden ants and carpenter ants, like sweet things. No matter what ants eat, as adults they swallow only liquid. They squeeze the liquid out of their food and spit out the solid part.

Body and Senses

Like all insects, the ant has a tough outer covering called an EXOSKELETON, which gives it support and protection. Also, like all insects, the ant has six legs and breathes air through tiny openings in the exoskeleton. Its body has three parts: head, thorax, and abdomen.

The Ant as a Movie Star   We have all seen monster movies featuring giant ant-like creatures attacking seemingly defenseless humans. The image of a giant ant head with long ANTENNAE has led to many a nightmare. In reality, the ant uses its antennae to touch, smell, taste,

This queen green ant, like all ants, has a three-part body with a tough skeleton on the outside.

This Eciton army ant soldier is in a threat pose, ready to defend its colony against attack.

hear, and "talk" to other ants. The anten- Central American rain forests, are blind.

nae wave in the air to pick up odors, tap The ant has two sets of jaws. It uses the

on objects to identify them, and touch the powerful front jaws to carry food, baby

ground to find the way. ants, and building materials. It can carry

The ant has two eyes on either side of up to 50 times its own weight! The front

its head. Most ants don't see very well, jaws are also used to dig and fight. The ant

and a few species, such as the *Prionopelta* of chews with the second set of jaws.

This common black carpenter ant, like all ants, has six strong, running legs and two long antennae.

Thorax Power   The THORAX (chest) powers the ant's six strong, running legs. Two hooked claws on the ends help the ant walk upside down on branches or ceilings.

The thorax also supports the two pairs of wings on the males and young queens. These are the only ants that have wings.

The Community Stomach   The ant's slender, oval ABDOMEN is made up of the waist and GASTER. The waist connects the thorax to the gaster. The ant's thin waist helps it bend easily when crawling through tunnels.

The gaster contains the ant's stomach

and glands that produce PHEROMONES, or chemical odors used to communicate. Some species also have a poison gland. The poison is ejected through a stinger or through an opening at the end of the ant's abdomen.

The stomachs of queens and workers are made up of two parts. The first part, called a CROP, is a social stomach where the ant stores liquid food for itself and other ants. When another ant is hungry, it touches a worker's head with its antennae. The worker spits up food from its crop and passes it into the hungry ant's mouth. A worker's crop can feed up to eight others!

Ants Come in All Sizes

Ants are usually yellow, brown, red, or black, and a few shine like metal. Some ants are as tiny as a dot and others are more than 1 inch (2.5 cm) long. For example, an entire colony of the tiny *Brachymyrmex* found in South America could live inside the head of a soldier of the giant Bornean carpenter ant (*Camponotus gigas*).

It's an Ant's Life

The ant's life, like that of most insects, has four stages: egg, larva, pupa, and adult. This process of growth is called METAMORPHOSIS, which means "change in form." In ants, the process takes one to four months, depending on the weather and species.

Queens Lay Eggs Only certain female ants lay eggs. As babies, these future queens are fed special food by worker ants so they will produce eggs. In most species, young queens also grow wings. Most male ants also have wings. The winged males and females fly only at mating time.

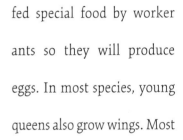

This queen is much larger than the workers, because her body contains hundreds of eggs.

Mating usually takes place during the warm summer months. This is an exciting, frantic time in the nest. The young queens and males fly out from their nests, often in swarms.

The mating flight is very important to the future of the colony. If it is missed or something goes wrong, there will be no new babies. During mating, the female gets enough sperm from the male to last her lifetime. His job done, the male dies within a few days.

17

The young queen's job is just beginning. She uses her legs to snap off her wings. Then, all alone, she hunts for a safe place to dig a nest, often under a stone or log. During this time, she is in a lot of danger from enemies such as spiders and other ants. Scientists estimate that only one in 500 young queens succeed in starting a new colony.

After the new queen digs a nest, she seals the entrance. Then she lays a small batch of eggs. She lives off the fat and nutrients stored in her wing muscles.

The new queen's eggs will develop into workers. Later, when the colony is more established, she will lay eggs that develop into winged females, winged males, and soldiers. Eggs that the queen fertilizes with sperm become females, and unfertilized eggs produce males.

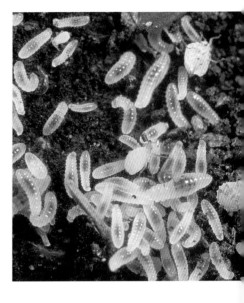

These baby ants called larvae look like tiny white worms. They don't have legs and are blind and helpless.

The Larva is an Eating Machine   Each egg hatches into a LARVA, a white, worm-like creature with no legs. It is blind and helpless. The queen feeds it with saliva and special eggs that she lays for food.

The larva is an eating machine, so its skin soon gets too tight. No problem! The larva splits its skin and crawls out, a process of growth called MOLTING. The larva molts four or five times.

Pupa—Big Change Inside   The last time the larva sheds its skin, it is ready for another change. In most species, the larva spins a COCOON, or protective cover, around itself. The cocoon is white and looks much like the egg, but bigger. It is now a PUPA. As it rests, the pupa slowly becomes an adult ant.

Inside these cocoons, the larvae are changing into adult ants. When an ant is ready to come out, it bites a hole in its cocoon.

Adult—Time to Work When the new ant's change is complete, it bites a hole in its cocoon. The queen ant helps make the hole larger. The new ant is pale and soft, but it soon will get darker and its skin will harden.

The new ants go to work immediately. They dig out of the nest to get food for the queen and each other. From now on, all the queen will do is lay eggs. The workers will care for her and shower attention on the new babies. The colony will grow faster now that the queen has workers to help her.

How Ants "Talk"

To live and work together in such large families, ants need to "talk" to one another. How do they do it?

Simple messages are easy. Most ant species simply tap or stroke one another with their antennae, as you would tap a

friend on the shoulder. Hungry ants tap worker ants to share their food.

Ants also "talk" with sounds. Most kinds make a high-pitched squeak by rubbing a scraper on their waist against ridges on their abdomen. This

A queen and a worker ant touch their antennae to "talk" to one another.

Many ants collect sweet juices from flowers. They store what they don't need in their crops to share with other ants.

is called STRIDULATION. For example, the leafcutter ant squeaks to get other ants to join her when she finds the right kind of leaf.

Odor Messages The most common way ants talk is with pheromones, or chemical odors. Ants use between 10 and 20 chemical "words" and "phrases." For example, ants can tell their nestmates from strangers by their odor.

Ants also use chemical odors to make trails. When a worker ant finds food, it drags the tip of its abdomen along the ground as it returns to the nest. This leaves an odor trail that other ants follow to the food.

Chemical odors also signal alarm. When enemies attack the nest, the first ants to fight release a chemical that attracts other workers to the battle.

These ants have attracted their nestmates to help fight enemy invaders by giving off an odor called a pheromone.

These Azteca ants live a fairly common ant life inside a hollow plant stem, but some ants have amazing lifestyles.

Lifestyles of Ants

All ants live and work together in communities. But the day-to-day lives of the communities differ greatly. Most ants build nests, but army ants, for example, live in temporary camps. At night they link their bodies together to form a large ball. In the center is a safe, warm chamber for the queen and babies.

Let's peek into some other amazing ant nests.

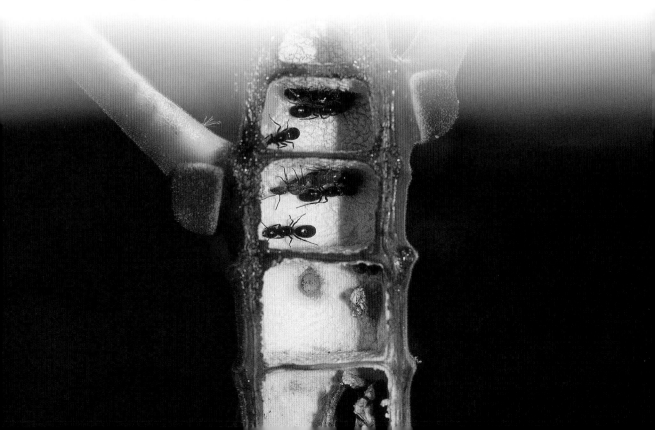

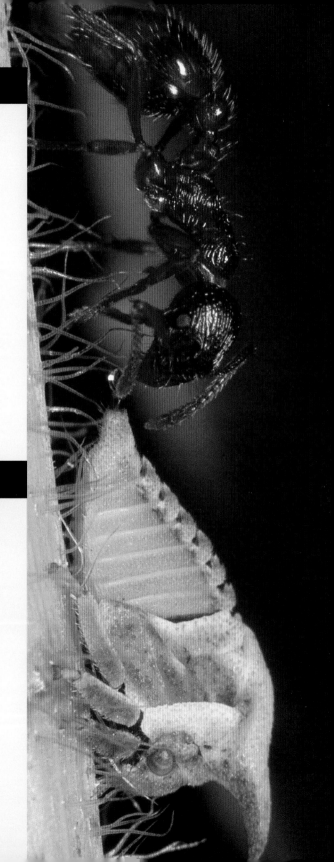

Ants and Aphid "Cows"

Many kinds of ants, such as *Lasius*, tend herds of aphid "cows" and other tiny insect "cows." Aphids are tiny insects that suck sap from plants. They squirt out the nutrients they don't use as a sweet liquid called honeydew. The ant milks its "cows" by stroking the aphid's abdomen with its antennae. The aphid then squirts out a drop of honeydew.

The ant "milks" many aphids, filling its crop (upper stomach) with the sweet liquid. In return, the ants protect the aphids from enemies like the ladybug, and sometimes even keep the aphid eggs in their nest during the winter.

Weaver Ants—Tree Nesters

The *Oecophylla* weaver ants build their nests with leaves and silk thread high up in tropical forests in Africa, Asia, and Australia. Hundreds of worker ants pull two leaves together with their legs and jaws. Other workers "glue" the leaves together with silk threads.

Where do they get the silk? Workers pick up larvae that are ready to spin silk cocoons. They carry the babies gently in their jaws and move them back and forth across the leaf edges. The larvae squirt out threads of silk that stick together to make a "glue."

Leafcutter Ants—The Farmers

In the forests of Central and South America, leafcutter ants called *Atta* grow fungus gardens in their underground nests. Large workers cut pieces of leaves from trees with their scissors-like jaws. They march single file back to the nest carrying the leaf pieces above their heads.

Back at the nest, smaller workers chew up the leaves and add them to the garden. A fluffy white fungus or mold grows on top of the leaves. Still smaller workers tend the garden and carry tufts of the fungus to their nestmates to eat.

Ant Enemies

Spiders, frogs, toads, lizards, birds, and many kinds of insects PREY on, or hunt, ants. The anteaters of tropical America tear open ant nests with their long, sharp claws. They often eat a whole nest of ants with their long, sticky tongues.

Ants protect themselves by biting, stinging, or spraying poison. All ants can bite, and about half of all species have a sting. The sting releases a painful, gooey poison that can gum up the antennae, legs, or jaws of another insect.

This young queen has been caught by a jumping spider before she could start a new nest.

Ant Wars

Ants are the most warlike of all creatures. They constantly fight other colonies, even the same species, over food or territory. Some feuds go on for years. The fierce battles are usually fought to the death.

What are their battle tactics? In the southern United States, soldiers of the woodland ant *(Pheidole dentata)* use their jaws as clippers to cut off the legs and heads of the red imported fire ant *(Solenopsis invicta)*. In the southwestern desert, workers of *Conomyrma bicolor* drop pebbles into the nests of honeypot ants. The European thief ant *(Solenopsis fugax)* squirts a poison-like pepper spray into the nests of other species.

Ants and Us

A few kinds of ants are pests. They join our picnics and come into our homes. Carpenter ants sometimes destroy wooden homes with their tunnels. The aphid "cows" protected by *Lasius* ants destroy corn and other crops. Leafcutter ants strip leaves from fruit trees on tropical plantations.

Some kinds of ants also have bites or stings strong enough to cause pain in humans. One is the red imported fire ant. Its sting burns like fire. A few people are highly allergic to the sting.

Ants Are Our Friends   In spite of their bad reputation, the trillions of ants on the earth play a very important role in all cycles of life, including our own. For example, ants are the chief predators of insects and spiders, many of which are pests in fields, gardens, and orchards. Scientists

As this Formica worker collects nectar from a flower, she gets covered with pollen.

have counted 102,000 insects carried back to a wood ant nest in one hour!

For centuries, Chinese citrus growers have tied nests of weaver ants to their mandarin orange trees. The ants protect the trees and fruit from other insects and hungry animals.

Just about any square yard of earth

contains an ant colony. Ants move even more soil than earthworms! The ants' tunnels let in air and loosen the soil.

Ants are also the world's cemetery squad. They collect more than 90 percent of the dead bodies of creatures their size and carry them back to their nests for food.

Ants are both helpful and harmful, but overall we couldn't live without them. Their trillions of lives are closely woven with ours. Without them, our planet would not be the same.

Ants feed on many insects. These Pheidole workers pull a cockroach nymph back to their nest.

L E A R N I N G   R E S O U R C E S

BEST BOOKS

The Ants, Burt Hölldobler and Edward O. Wilson, The Belknap Press of Harvard University Press, 1990, Pulitzer Prize winner

Journey to the Ants, Burt Hölldobler and Edward O. Wilson, The Belknap Press of Harvard University Press, 1994

MORE BOOKS

Ant, Michael Chinery, Troll Associates, 1991

An Ant Colony, Heiderose and Andreas Fischer-Nagel, Carolrhoda Books, 1989

Ants, Cynthia Overbeck, Lerner Publications Company, 1982, adapted from *Ants and Their World*, 1971

Ants, Edward S. Ross, The Child's World, 1995

Ants, a Great Community, Secrets of the Animal World, Andreu Llamas, Gareth Stevens Publishing, 1996

Life of the Ant, Jun Nanao, Raintree Publishers, 1986, translated from *The Daily Life of the Ant*, 1973

Looking at Ants, Dorothy Hinshaw Patent (Ph.D. in zoology), Holiday House, 1989

WEB

"The Ants," Gordon's Entomological Home Page

"Control of the Red Imported Fire Ant," North Carolina Cooperative Extension Service

"Imported Fire Ants," Timothy C. Lockley, Imported Fire Ant Station, The University of Minnesota

"Of Ants & Men," Edward O. Wilson

ENCYCLOPEDIAS AND REFERENCE BOOKS

Academic American Encyclopedia, 1992, William H. Gotwald, Jr. (entomologist)

Compton's Encyclopedia online

Encyclopedia Americana, 1985

Encyclopedia of Animal Life, The Audubon Society, 1982, pp. 471–477

Groliers online, William H. Gotwald, Jr. (entomologist)

Grzimek's Animal Encyclopedia, Vol. 2, Insects, 1975, pp. 441–455

The Illustrated Encyclopedia of Wildlife, 1991, pp. 2551–2564

National Audubon Society Field Guide to North American Insects & Spiders, 1995

World Book Encyclopedia, 1996

MAGAZINE ARTICLES

"The Ant Man," *Boys' Life*, Lynn O'Shaughnessy, June 1996, pp. 20–25

"Picnic Spoilers and Nature Balancers," Marilyn Pokorney, *World & I*, April 1995, pp. 202+

MUSEUMS

Coyote Point Museum
San Mateo, CA

The Discovery Center
Fort Lauderdale, FL

Milwaukee Public Museum
Milwaukee, WI

Smithsonian Institution
Washington, DC

I N D E X